RSVP: THE DIRECTORY OF ILLUSTRATION & DESIGN IS PUBLISHED BY RICHARD LEBENSON AND KATHLEEN CREIGHTON, P.O. BOX 050314, BROOKLYN, NY 11205

VOL. 20, NO.1 • ISBN # 1-878118-04-8

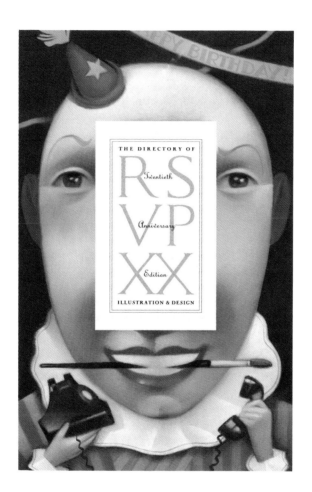

THE DIRECTORY OF

RSVP

Twentieth
Anniversary
Edition

XX

ILLUSTRATION & DESIGN

CREDITS

PUBLISHER: RICHARD LEBENSON & KATHLEEN CREIGHTON • **COORDINATION/ SALES**: RICHARD LEBENSON • **DESIGN & PROMOTION**: KATHLEEN CREIGHTON & STEPHEN BODKIN • **BUSINESS & PROMOTION**: JOE GREENSTEIN • **OFFICE MANAGER**: HARVEY WILSON • **SALES**: PAUL KRAUSS • **TRAFFIC**: FRANK ATTONG **COVER ILLUSTRATION**: GARY KELLEY **COVER DESIGN**: LOUISE FILI • **TYPESETTING**: BCD INK, LTD. • **PRODUCTION**: JOHN CLEVELAND • **THANKS TO**: TONY BRUSCO, AL DE ANGELO, DOMENICK DI GIACOMO, JUAN HUNT, ALAN KOCHIS, KATHY ORR, FRANK ROSSINI, GARY STAHL, RON WEIR **PRINTING**: AGT/FLEETWOOD LITHO

CONTENTS

RSVP 20 FEATURES THE WORK OF 253 ARTISTS, ILLUSTRATORS AND DESIGNERS NATIONWIDE • INDEXED ALPHABETICALLY BY SPECIFIC SKILLS, AND BY REGION IN OUR GEOGRAPHIC INDEX • RSVP CALLBACK® 718/857-9267, OUR 24 HOUR, 7 DAY/WEEK ANSWERING SERVICE • (SEE PAGE 320 FOR COMPLETE DETAILS)

RSVP 20: EVERYTHING STARTS WITH A VISION. AND EVERY VISION TAKES A LOT OF HARD WORK AND A LOT OF LUCK TO DEVELOP INTO SOMETHING LASTING AND WORTHWHILE.

TWENTY YEARS AGO WE SAW AN OPPORTUNITY TO HELP BOTH ARTISTS AND ART BUYERS. WE STEPPED INTO THE VOID THAT EXISTED AND HELPED FORGE AN INDUSTRY AROUND SELF-PROMO-TION AND NETWORKING THAT HAS BECOME SUCH AN INTEGRAL PART OF THE WAY PEOPLE DO BUSINESS TODAY IN THE FIELD OF COMMUNICATIONS.

SO, WE TAKE PARTICULAR PLEASURE IN LOOKING BACK OVER OUR 20 YEARS IN THE BUSINESS. IT'S TIME TO CELEBRATE, TO REFLECT ON OUR ACCOMPLISH-MENTS, BUT MORE, A TIME TO LOOK TO THE FUTURE WITH THE SAME EXCITEMENT AND VISION THAT WE STARTED WITH.

The RSVP staff: Kathleen Creighton, Harvey Wilson, Frank Attong, Joe Greenstein, Richard Lebens

ON THE OCCASION OF OUR 20TH ANNIVERSARY, WE AT

WOULD LIKE TO THANK YOU FOR MAKING IT ALL POSSIBLE.

NOW THAT YOU'VE SEEN US

WE'D LIKE TO SEE YOU.

INTRODUCING

THE RSVP20
COMPETITION

ANNOUNCING CALL FOR ENTRIES

ARTISTS

SELF•PORTRAIT

COMPETITION

IN KEEPING WITH RSVP'S 20-YEAR CELEBRATION OF THE CREATIVE SPIRIT, WE ARE PLEASED TO ANNOUNCE A UNIQUE COMPETITION, OPEN TO ALL ARTISTS. THE THEME IS SELF-PORTRAITS, AND WE ENCOURAGE YOU TO INTERPRET THIS SUBJECT IN ANY STYLE AND MANNER THAT BEST COMMUNICATES YOU TO US.

☛ WHO'S ELIGIBLE: ILLUSTRATORS, DESIGNERS, ART DIRECTORS, FINE ARTISTS & STUDENTS

DEADLINE FOR ENTRY: JUNE 30, 1995

FORMAT FOR ENTRIES: TRANSPARENCIES (35MM OR LARGER FORMAT) OR COMPUTER GENERATED (POSITIVE) MATCH PRINTS. ALL ENTRIES MUST BE LABELED WITH ARTIST'S NAME AT FRONT TOP.

ENTRY FEE: $12 FOR FIRST ENTRY SUBMITTED, $5 FOR EACH ADDITIONAL SUBMISSION

PRIZES: FIRST PRIZE: $1000 IN CASH, SECOND PRIZE: $500 IN CASH, THIRD PRIZE: $250 IN CASH. ALL PRIZES INCLUDE A FULL-COLOR REPRODUCTION OF YOUR SELF-PORTRAIT IN RSVP21.

• JUDGES •
LOUISE FILI, GRAPHIC DESIGNER
RICHARD LEBENSON, PUBLISHER, RSVP
MEL ODOM, ILLUSTRATOR

A SPECIAL GALLERY SECTION OF RSVP21 WILL SHOWCASE THE ENTRIES OF THE GRAND PRIZE WINNERS, AS WELL AS ENTRIES BY SELECTED FINALISTS. THESE ARTISTS WILL ALSO BE INVITED TO PARTICIPATE IN AN ARTIST'S SELF-PORTRAITS EXHIBITION TO BE MOUNTED BY RSVP IN NEW YORK CITY IN 1996.

HOW TO ENTER: SEND YOUR ENTRY PLUS CHECK OR MONEY ORDER (PAYABLE TO RSVP) TO: RSVP20 COMPETITION, P.O. BOX 050314, BROOKLYN, NY 11205. (THOSE WISHING THEIR SUBMISSIONS RETURNED MUST INCLUDE A STAMPED, SELF-ADDRESSED ENVELOPE.)

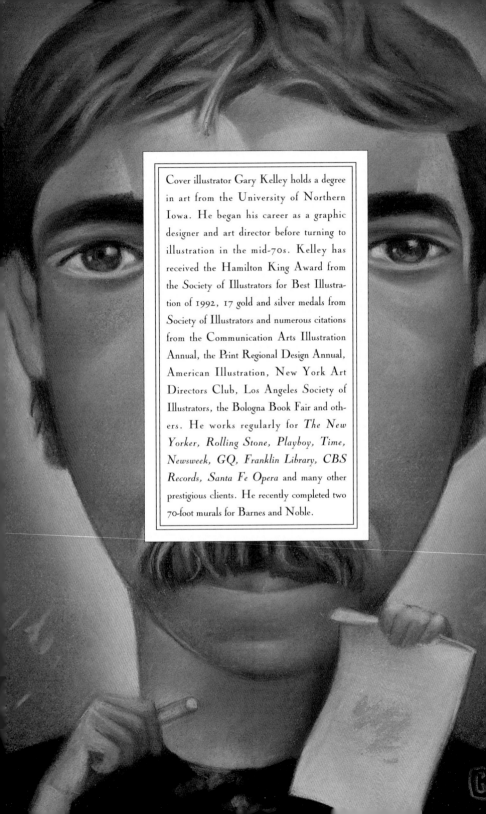

Cover illustrator Gary Kelley holds a degree in art from the University of Northern Iowa. He began his career as a graphic designer and art director before turning to illustration in the mid-70s. Kelley has received the Hamilton King Award from the Society of Illustrators for Best Illustration of 1992, 17 gold and silver medals from Society of Illustrators and numerous citations from the Communication Arts Illustration Annual, the Print Regional Design Annual, American Illustration, New York Art Directors Club, Los Angeles Society of Illustrators, the Bologna Book Fair and others. He works regularly for *The New Yorker, Rolling Stone, Playboy, Time, Newsweek, GQ, Franklin Library, CBS Records, Santa Fe Opera* and many other prestigious clients. He recently completed two 70-foot murals for Barnes and Noble.

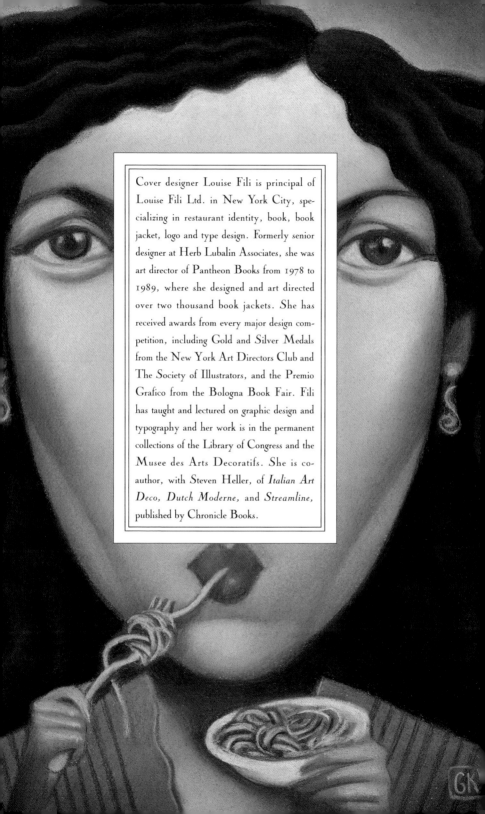

Cover designer Louise Fili is principal of Louise Fili Ltd. in New York City, specializing in restaurant identity, book, book jacket, logo and type design. Formerly senior designer at Herb Lubalin Associates, she was art director of Pantheon Books from 1978 to 1989, where she designed and art directed over two thousand book jackets. She has received awards from every major design competition, including Gold and Silver Medals from the New York Art Directors Club and The Society of Illustrators, and the Premio Grafico from the Bologna Book Fair. Fili has taught and lectured on graphic design and typography and her work is in the permanent collections of the Library of Congress and the Musee des Arts Decoratifs. She is co-author, with Steven Heller, of *Italian Art Deco, Dutch Moderne,* and *Streamline,* published by Chronicle Books.

ILLUSTRATION

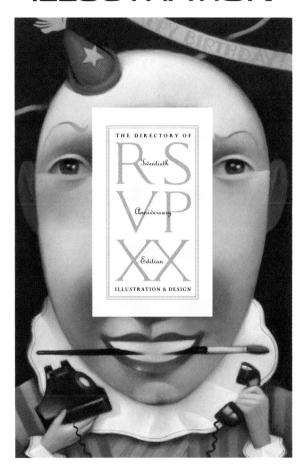

THE DIRECTORY OF

R S
V P
X X

Twentieth

Anniversary

Edition

ILLUSTRATION & DESIGN

MICHAEL J. DEAS
Represented by the Newborn Group
(212) 260–6700

Maria Jimenez

33-34 77th Street, # 6F, Jackson Hts., N.Y. 11372
(718) 424-7727

P A L E N C A R

J O H N   J U D E   P A L E N C A R

249 ELM STREET, OBERLIN, OHIO 44074 • (216) 774-7312

JOHN MONTELEONE
CALL CHRIS PETERSON ARTISTS REPRESENTATIVE
(516) 747-3035 • FAX (516) 739-3556 • STUDIO (516) 431-3061
SEE ALSO WORKBOOK 93 & 94

MARK FREDRICKSON

5093 East Patricia Street • Tucson, Arizona 85712

6 0 2 • 3 2 3 • 3 1 7 9

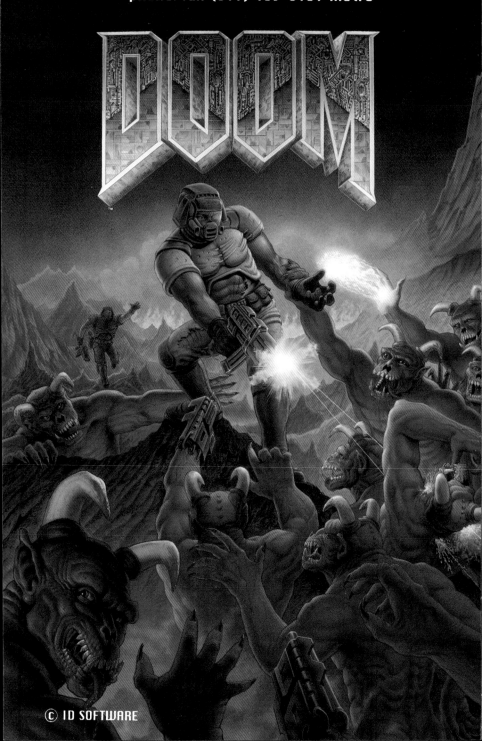

MITCHELL HEINZE
721 E MAXWELL LANE
LATHROP CA 95330
209 • 858 • 1131

JOE DICESARE

5A NINTH STREET BROOKLYN, NY 11215 (718) 499-9025

JOEL
SPECTOR

JOEL SPECTOR • 3 MAPLEWOOD DRIVE
NEW MILFORD, CT 06776 • 203 355-5942 • 203 355-537

MEL ODOM

ILLUSTRATION

212 724-9320

RODERICK KARMENZIND

102 SOUTH SECOND STREET, SUITE 207, DE KALB, IL
PHONE (815)758-4743 VOICE MAIL (815)748-6364 FAX AVAILABLE UPON REQUEST

RENÉ MILOT

Renard Represents • tel (212) 490-2450 • fax (212) 697-6828

ROBERT RODRIGUEZ

Renard Represents • tel (212)490-2450 • fax (212)697-6828

VALERIE SINCLAIR

Renard Represents • tel (212) 490-2450 • fax (212) 697-6828

BILL CIGLIANO

Renard Represents • tel (212)490-2450 • fax (212)697-6828

KAZUHIKO SANO

Renard Represents • tel (212)490-2450 • fax (212)697-6828

© 1994 STEVE BJORKMAN

STEVE BJÖRKMAN

Renard Represents • tel(212)490-2450 • fax(212)697-6828

DAN GARROW

Renard Represents • tel(212)490-2450 • fax(212)697-6828

JEFFREY PELO

Renard Represents • tel (212) 490-2450 • fax (212) 697-6828

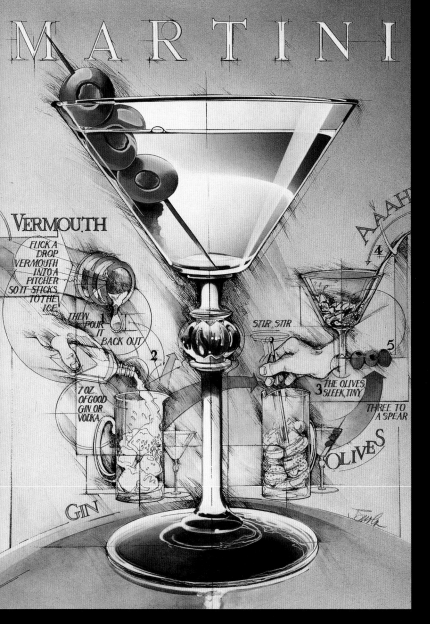

MARTINI

VERMOUTH

FLICK A
DROP
VERMOUTH
INTO A
PITCHER
SO IT STICKS
TO THE
ICE

THEN
POUR
IT
BACK OUT

7 OZ.
OF GOOD
GIN OR
VODKA

STIR, STIR

THE OLIVES,
SLEEK, TINY,

THREE TO
A SPEAR

GIN

OLIVES

AAAH

JIM SMOLA

ILLUSTRATION   (203) 665-0305

94 MAPLE HILL AVE. NEWINGTON, CT 06111

G A R Y K E L L E Y

R E P R E S E N T E D   B Y

R I C H A R D   S O L O M O N

2   1   2   -   6   8   3   -   1   6   3   2

CREIGHTON

CAMERON CLEMENT
NATIONAL GRAPHIC EXPLORER
(501) 646-7734

Gary Hallgren

98 LAURELTON DRIVE
MASTIC BEACH, NY 11951
516 399-5531

THE WALL STREET JOURNAL • THE NEW YORK TIMES • ESQUIRE
AMERICAN EXPRESS • FORBES • NEW YORK • BUSINESS WEEK • FORTUNE
ENTERTAINMENT WEEKLY • NEWSWEEK • MARVEL COMICS

Stu Suchit

(201) 963-3011
RSVP CALLBACK ANSWERING SERVICE (718) 857-9267

YASUO TANAKA

212 995 8489

Illustration, Calligraphy, Puzzles & Curiosities
Leah Palmer PREISS 919·833·8443
for a partial list of clients look closely at the border

Tiul'panoff

RSVP CALLBACK ANSWERING SERVICE (718) 857-9267

ED RENDELL, PHILADELPHIA'S MAYOR FOR INQUIRER

NUREYEV, ANTHONY HOPKINS AND THE PENQUIN

REBEKAH BOYER · ILLUSTRATOR · 215−271−9107

505 COURT STREET, APT. 4H, BROOKLYN, N.Y. 11231
(718) 852-8987

Alan Rabinowitz

5 1 6 - 2 2 1 - 9 8 9 7

2898 Mandalay Beach Road, Wantagh, NY 11793

Darryl Ligasan

212 · 889 · 502○

151 EAST 31ST STREET, 6B, NEW YORK CITY, NY 10016

BRUCE WALDMAN

18 WESTBROOK ROAD, WESTFIELD, NJ 07090
(908) 232-2840, RSVP CALLBACK ANSWERING SERVICE (718) 857-9267

HEIDE OBERHEIDE
121 OLD MAIN SHORE ROAD, WARETOWN, NJ 08758
609-693-1608

TWELVETREES
STUDIOS

216-261-2505

RSVP Callback answering service (718) 857-9267

R I C H   G R O T E

609-586-5896

21 TYNDALE RD., HAMILTON SQUARE, N.J. 08690
RSVP CALLBACK SERVICE (718)-857-9267

K E N • S P E N G L E R

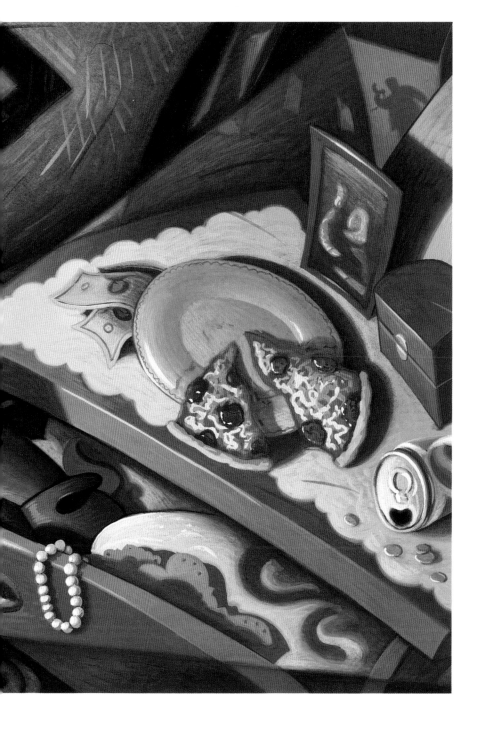

(9 1 6) 4 4 1 • 1 9 3 2

▉ David Lui ▉

▉LES MINTZ REPRESENTS, INC.
▉Tel: (212) 479-1771 Fax: (212) 479-1772
▉Tel: (305) 454-6566 Fax: (305) 454-6515

▮ Bernard Bonhomme ▮

▮LES MINTZ REPRESENTS, INC.
▮ Tel: (212) 479-1771 Fax: (212) 479-1772
▮ Tel: (305) 454-6566 Fax: (305) 454-6515

∎ Robert Bergin ∎

∎ LES MINTZ REPRESENTS, INC.
∎ Tel: (212) 479-1771 Fax: (212) 479-1772
∎ Tel: (305) 454-6566 Fax: (305) 454-6515

▮ Moline-Kramer ▮

■ Val Johnson ■

■ LES MINTZ REPRESENTS, INC.
■ Tel: (212) 479-1771 Fax: (212) 479-1772
■ Tel: (305) 454-6566 Fax: (305) 454-6515

▌ Mike Gushock ▌

▌LES MINTZ REPRESENTS, INC.
▌Tel: (212) 479-1771 Fax: (212) 479-1772
▌Tel: (305) 454-6566 Fax: (305) 454-6515

RICHARD MURDOCK ILLUSTRATIONS
225 Maple Road, Easton, CT 06612 (203) 261-3042

ALEX EBEL

30 NEWPORT ROAD, YONKERS, NEW YORK 10710 (914) 961-4058

65

STUDIO
708.447.4454

GREGORY HERGERT

DARRYL ZUDECK

35 WEST 92ND ST., NY, NY 10025
(212) 663-9454

S.B. WHITEHEAD ∷ ILLUSTRATION

KI RK

RICHARD KIRK
(508) 883-2838

RICHARD KIRK
(5 0 8) 8 8 3 - 2 8 3 8

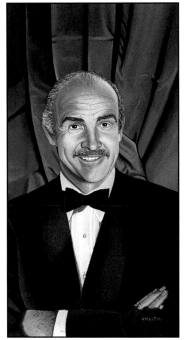

R . M A R T I N

RICHARD MARTIN • PO BOX 268, WANTAGH, NY 11793 • (516) 377-3844
RSVP CALLBACK ANSWERING SERVICE (718) 857-9267

AMY J. GRIGG

25 HIGHMEADOW LANE • ENFIELD, CT. 06082

203 • 763 • 1705

DAN KROVATIN

(609) 895 - 1634

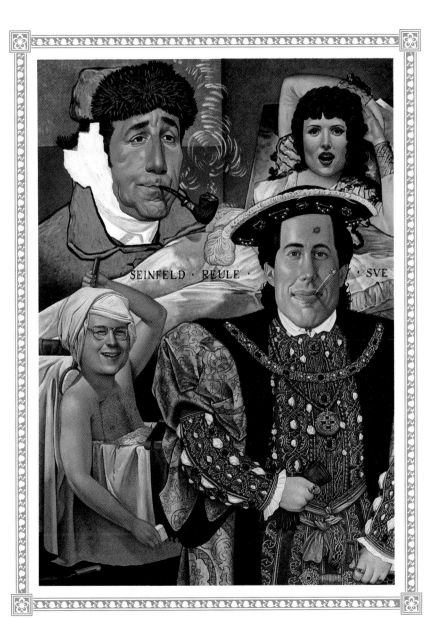

SEINFELD · REULE · SVE

ROBERTO PARADA

142 CANTERBURY AVENUE • N. ARLINGTON, N.J. 07031 • 201-998-0922

Clients include: Playgirl, Tthe Daily News, Personal Selling Power, Georgette Mosbacher, National Review, Medical Labratory Observer

ALEXANDER BLOCH
139 EAST 33RD STREET, #3E, N.Y., N.Y. 10016
PHONE/FAX (212) 532-3374

PHIL FOSTER

615 - 895 - 1114

528 Independence Way, Murfreesboro, TN 37129

Joe Baker

PHOTO–MONTAGE PHOTOGRAPHY, 35 WOOSTER ST./SOHO, N.Y., N.Y. 10013
OIL AND COLORED PENCIL ON BLACK AND WHITE PHOTOGRAPHS
(212) 925–6555

Joe Baker

PHOTO–MONTAGE PHOTOGRAPHY, 35 WOOSTER ST./SOHO, N.Y., N.Y. 10013
OIL AND COLORED PENCIL ON BLACK AND WHITE PHOTOGRAPHS
(212) 925-6555

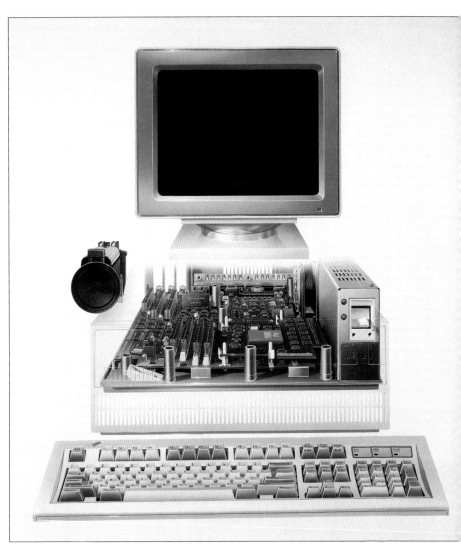

TERRANCE J. RYAN

REPRESENTED BY TOM PRITCHETT
247 WEST 10TH STREET, #1-A, NEW YORK, NY 10014
TEL 212•688•1080   FAX 519•735•7177

CLIENTS: GILLETTE CO., LINCOLN-MERCURY, RAVEL-MONOGRAM INC., FORD ELECTRONICS, WALL STREET JOURNAL, USA TODAY, POPULAR MECHANICS, READERS DIGEST, J. WALTER THOMPSON, YOUNG & RUBRICAM, THOMPSON INTERNATIONAL, STROH'S BEER, PEACHSTATE MOTORSPORTS, ACCURATE MINIATURES, SCIENTIFIC AMERICAN, HOME MECHANIX, ATLAS COPCO, POPULAR SCIENCE, BOATING MAGAZINE, RC/BBD&O, McCANN-ERICKSON, BACKER, SPIELVOGEL & BATES, OGILVY & MATHER

Steve Brennan

Artists   89   New York   212
Representative   Fifth Avenue   New York   627-1554
         Suite 901   10003   627-1719 Fax

RSVP CALLBACK ANSWERING SERVICE (718) 857-9267

Charles Thomas

6 0 2 · 7 4 3 · 3 6 1 3

Dino Massaroni

216-929-0431

Rodney Jung

67-14 108TH STREET, 2A, FOREST HILLS, NY 11375
(718) 544-4278 🐢 FAX (718) 544-3341

BRIAN HARROLD

AIRBRUSH ILLUSTRATION (212) 661 - 4568

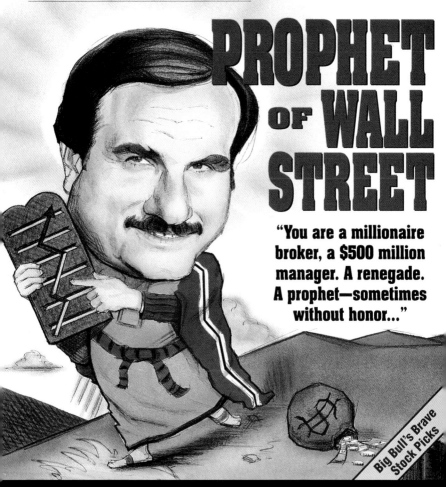

AIN'T THE FREE MARKET GRAND?
MLP Tax Bonanza

NO-LOADERS DON'T TELL THE TRUTH
New Study Reveals Load Funds' Edge

BEWARE THE STEALTH TAX
"Success Tax" Strikes Big Earners

FINANCIAL PLANNING
On WALL STREET

Insights & Analysis for Successful Brokers & Managers

May 1994
$8.00

PROPHET OF WALL STREET

"You are a millionaire broker, a $500 million manager. A renegade. A prophet—sometimes without honor..."

Big Bull's Brave Stock Picks

CARICATURE BY FRED MARSHALL
420 EAST 70th STREET NEW YORK, N.Y. 10021
BUS: (212) 944-7771 • HOME: (212) 249-7041
RSVP CALLBACK ANSWERING SERVICE (718) 857-9267 SEE ALSO RSVP #19 pgs 24 & 25

AIRBRUSH

ILLUSTRATION

•

PLEASE SEE RSVP

13, 14, 15, 16, 1,8

FOR ADDITIONAL

SAMPLES

•

RSVP CALLBACK

ANSWERING SERVICE

(718) 857-9267

ROBERT ROPER

Jannine Cabossel
ILLUSTRATION

Studio: 505-983-4099 ✺ Santa Fe, New Mexico

TUKO FUJISAKI ILLUSTRATION

NEW YORK 718/789-7472

SAN DIEGO 619/276-0566

BETH ADAMS

Palace Tzigane
Budapest

Paris Chalet Blasé
Paris

Toupeé

Hjalmal

The Blissomore Hotel
New York

Hotel Tocororo
Cuba

415·648·0355

Represented by Irmeli Holmberg 212·545·9155

KIMBLE PENDLETON MEAD
125 PROSPECT PARK WEST, BROOKLYN, NY 11215
(718) 768-3632

JOEL F. NAPRSTEK

76 Park Pl, Morris Plains, NJ 07950
201-285-0692 / fax 201-267-1575

A Taste of the Holidays

Represented by Bill and Maurine KLJMT 212•799•2231

Pat Porter

Represented by Bill and Maurine KLIMT 212•799•

DELLA©

MCINTOSH

Represented by Bill and Maurine KLIMT 212•799•2231

Richard Pascucci
Illustrator
39 Wright Ave.
Lynbrook, N.Y. 11563
Studio # (516)887-3327

JONWEIMAN
I L L U S T R A T I O N

TEL 718.855.8468
FAX 718.855.5060
88 WYCKOFF ST 3C
BROOKLYN, NY
11201

STEPHEN SWENY (404) 299-7535 • RSVP CALLBACK (718) 857-9267

JOHN KANZLER ILLUSTRATION
203 • 782 • 6981
O LINDEN ST. NEW HAVEN, CT 06511

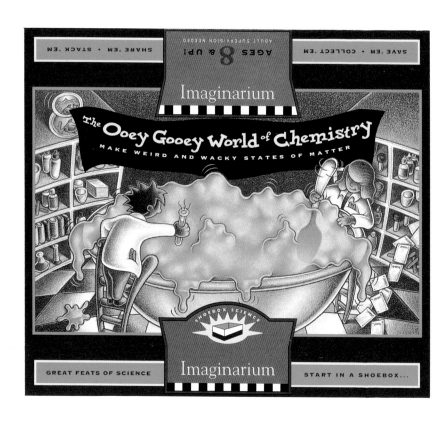

Gregg Valley

Phone: 412•941•4662 ☺ Fax: 412•941•3490

JIMMY HOLDER
ph: (818) 244-6707   fax: (818) 244-6766
1507 Columbia Drive Glendale, CA 91205

RICHARD WEISS
ILLUSTRATOR

215 567-3828

126 S. 22ND ST., PHILADELPHIA, PA 19103

STEVE HENRY

7 PARK AVENUE, NEW YORK, NY 10016
(212) 532-2487

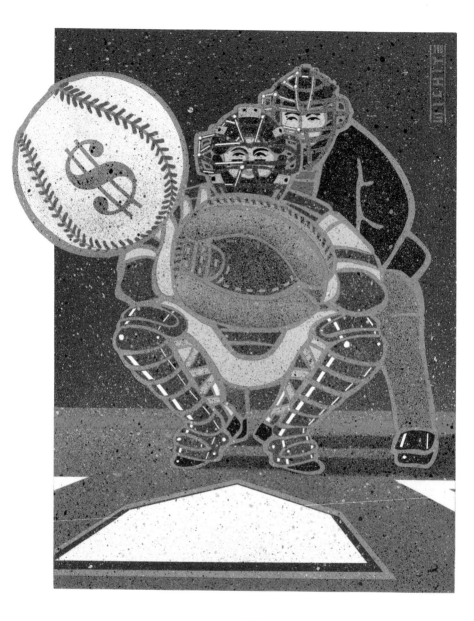

Dean Wilhite Design Company

ILLUSTRATION • DESIGN • TYPOGRAPHY

TELEPHONE 405.524.3326

GEORGE THOMPSON

433 WEST 43RD STREET #3E NYC 10036

PHONE & FAX 212.245.2543

RSVP CALLBACK ANSWERING SERVICE 718.857.9267

JOHN PAUL GENZO

3 EMILY COURT, ROBBINSVILLE, NJ 08691
609/259-6089   FAX 609/259-0398

CLIFFORD FAUST

NEW YORK CITY (212) 581-9461
RSVP CALLBACK ANSWERING SERVICE (718) 857-9267

ZINA SAUNDERS (212) 777-1201

JONAH HALL

(718) 383 7033

195 FRANKLIN ST., BROOKLYN, NY 11222

PLEASE CALL FOR A COMPLETE PORTFOLIO VIEWING

DENNIS HOCKERMAN

○

6024 W. CHAPEL HILL RD.
MEQUON, WISCONSIN 53097

(414) 242- 4103

Michael KUCHARSKI

CARLOS
TORRES
718 - 768 - 3296

C A R L O S
T O R R E S
7 1 8 - 7 6 8 - 3 2 9 6

STEPHEN HARRINGTON

255 WILTON ROAD WEST · RIDGEFIELD · CT · 06877
(203) 431 · 5854
REPRESENTED BY JOHN BREWSTER CREATIVE SERVICES

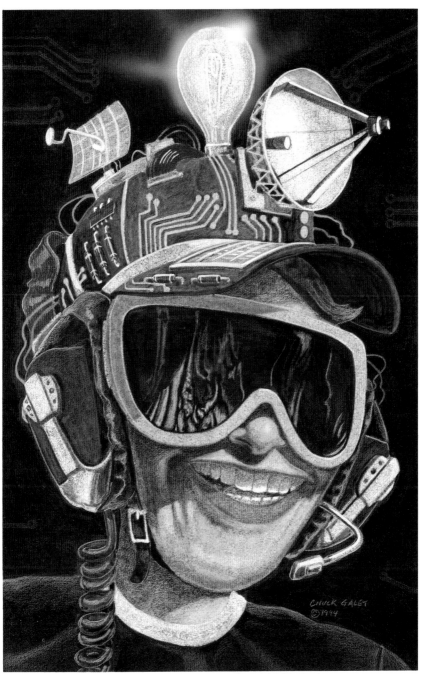

Chuck Galey
Humorous Illustration

601.373.6426 Studio phone & FAX
Represented by Andrea Lynch/Repertoire
214.369.6990 / 214.369.6938 (FAX)
See Creative Illustration '90, RSVP 18 & 19
for more samples.

BB SAMS
HUMOROUS ILLUSTRATION
(404) 464-2956

claudia newell
illustrations   **Call for a portfolio disk!**

718.384.5916 or 212.969.0795
151 first avenue.box 13.nyc.10003   e-mail: claudia@sensenet.com

Rick StroMoski

Illustrating Humorously

203·668·8738 Fax 203·668·8742

B.K. Taylor

24940 S. CROMWELL, FRANKLIN, MI 48025 (810) 626-8698 FAX (810) 855-8247
IN NY CONTACT IVY LEAGUE OF ARTISTS
156 FIFTH AVENUE, NEW YORK, NY 10010 (212) 243-1333

BRYNA WALDMAN

RSVP Call back answering service (718) 857-9267

F flea — fox

L O R E T T A   L U S T I G

330 CLINTON AVENUE, BROOKLYN, N.Y. 11205 (718) 789-2496

MaTt StRauB

(212) 995-9359   CALLBACK SERVICE:(718) 857-9267

PHILIP A. SCHEUER ● ILLUSTRATION ● 212-620-0728
126 FIFTH AVENUE ● NEW YORK CITY ● 10011

BILL MAYER, 240 FORKNER DRIVE, DECATUR, GA 30030 (404) 378-0686 FAX (404) 373-1759

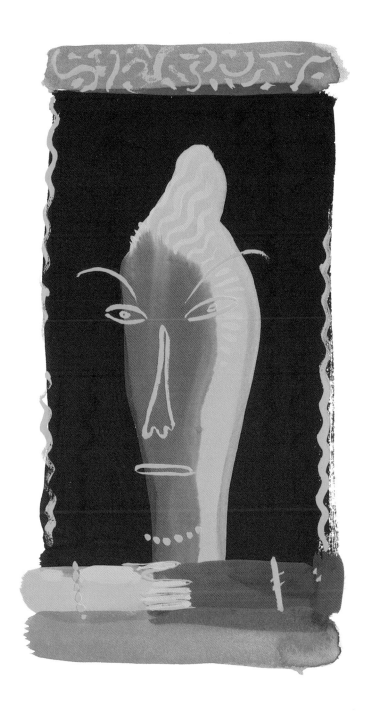

BILL MAYER, 240 FORKNER DRIVE, DECATUR, GA 30030 (404) 378-0686 FAX (404) 373-1759

Dave Nelson

illustration
6 0 3 · 5 6 3 · 8 2 6 7

125A Lower Jaffrey Road, Dublin, NH 03444

Global warming: Too late to stop?

Phone: 718·522·2335
Fax: 718·852·9109

Larry Johnson

When Jo Louis Won the Title

Belinda Rochelle Illustrated by Larry Johnson

· ARTISTS REPRESENTATIVE ·

· GWEN WALTERS ·

50 Fuller Brook Road · Wellesley, MA 02181

6 1 7 · 2 3 5 · 8 6 5 8

Gary Torrisi

· ARTISTS' REPRESENTATIVE ·
· GWEN WALTERS ·
50 Fuller Brook Road · Wellesley, MA 02181
6 1 7 · 2 3 5 · 8 6 5 8

Cheryl Roberts

Susan Spellman

ARTISTS' REPRESENTATIVE

· GWEN WALTERS ·

50 Fuller Brook Road · Wellesley, MA 02181

6 1 7 · 2 3 5 · 8 6 5 8

Pat Soper

Sally Schaedler

ARTISTS' REPRESENTATIVE

· GWEN WALTERS ·

50 Fuller Brook Road · Wellesley, MA 02181

6 1 7 · 2 3 5 · 8 6 5 8

135

Gary Phillips

ARTISTS' REPRESENTATIVE

· GWEN WALTERS ·

50 Fuller Brook Road · Wellesley, MA 02181

6 1 7 · 2 3 5 · 8 6 5 8

Joe Veno

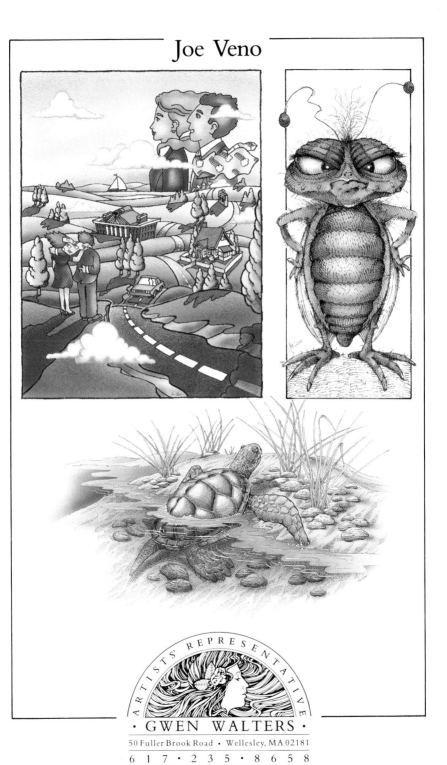

Stacey Schuett

Christina Tugeau (203) 438-7307

WHERE THE WAVES GROW SWEET
· DOUBT NOT REEPICHEEP ·
THERE IS THE UTTER EAST

DAVID SLONIM

Christina Tugeau   (203) 438-7307

Allan M. Burch

515 . 522 . 7826

RSVP callback answering
service 718 . 857 . 9267

ArtistS InternationaL

520 Bee Brook Road
Washington, Connecticut 06777
(205) 868-1011/FAX (205) 868-1272

Paul Lopez

FIRST AID

Rick Lieder

ILLUSTRATION

3653 Phillips ▪ Berkley ▪ MI ▪ 48072

810.544.0404

ELLEN THOMPSON

ILLUSTRATOR

908 422-0233

SEE ALSO RSVP 18 & 19
SOCIETY OF ILLUSTRATORS ANNUALS 28, 31 & 36

MARK COVELL

(203)228-1445

115 EAST STREET   HEBRON, CT   06248

▲ STEVE YOUNG – ROBONINER
DEION SANDERS OF THE ATLANTA FALCONS & BRAVES ▶

Wayne Anthony Still
215 - 635 - 2394

Wayne Anthony Still
215 - 635 - 2394

RIZZOLI PUBLICATIONS, INC.

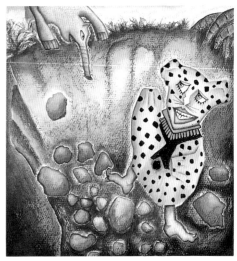

LIZA PAPI
Line, Wash, Woodcut, Linocut
231 W. 25th St. #3D • New York, NY 10001 • 212/627-7438

JILL BAUMAN

Illustration & Design

P.O. Box 150152, Kew Gardens, N.Y. 11415-0152 • (718) 886-5616

JG DESIGN

(718) 441-2321

REPRESENTING

LORENZ · Schleh

DONNA NAPOLI
ILLUSTRATION IN WATERCOLOR AND PASTELS
(718) 816-8769, OFFICE/FAX (718) 356-0513

HOLLIS ✶ BOGDANFFY
HUMOROUS ILLUSTRATION
212 832 8721 ✶ PHONE FAX MODEM

M.E. COHEN
357 WEST 12TH STREET • NEW YORK, NY 10014
PHONE (212) 627-8033 • FAX (212) 627-1167

DAVID BRION
28 CHEEVER PLACE, BROOKLYN, NY 11231
(718) 858-0362 • FAX (718) 596-4408

Christin Ranger

500 AURORA AVENUE NORTH #406C
SEATTLE, WASHINGTON 98109
(206) 682-2279 • FAX (206) 623-5008

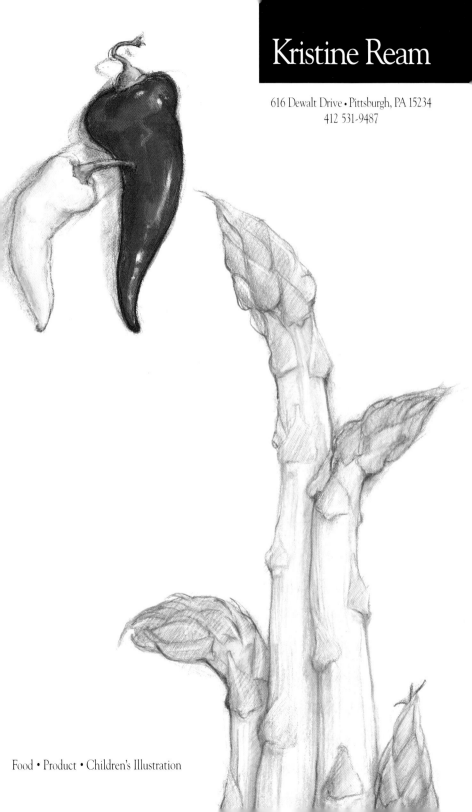

Kristine Ream

616 Dewalt Drive • Pittsburgh, PA 15234
412 531-9487

Food • Product • Children's Illustration

ARNIE TEN (914) 485-8419
RSVP CALLBACK ANSWERING SERVICE (718) 857-9267
FAX (914) 485-8419

DIANE N. STUBBS

COMPUTER ILLUSTRATION

3355 SPRING MOUNTAIN RD. • SUITE 19 • LAS VEGAS NV. 89102 • 702- 871-2711 FAX 702-871-5066

Robert Pasternak

114 West 27th St., New York City 10001
(212) 675-0002

AL HERING
914-471-7326

GUESS THE ANIMALS CONTEST!

Guess the number of animals and win a prize! Also, we'll send a Faxfolio immediately upon request! If you can't reach us call the RSVP Callback number: (718) 857-9267.

BARBARA GARRISON

12 EAST 87TH STREET, NEW YORK, N.Y. 10128
(212) 348-6382, RSVP CALLBACK ANSWERING SERVICE (718) 857-9267

JOHN RUGGERI
FOOD/COSMETICS/ACCESSORIES
AND PRODUCT RENDERINGS

245 EAST 19 STREET NYC 10003 212 979 6029

TATE NATION
803•884•9911

levinson

David Levinson · 86 Parson Road Apt#2 · Clifton · NJ 07012
Telephone · Fax (201)614-1627

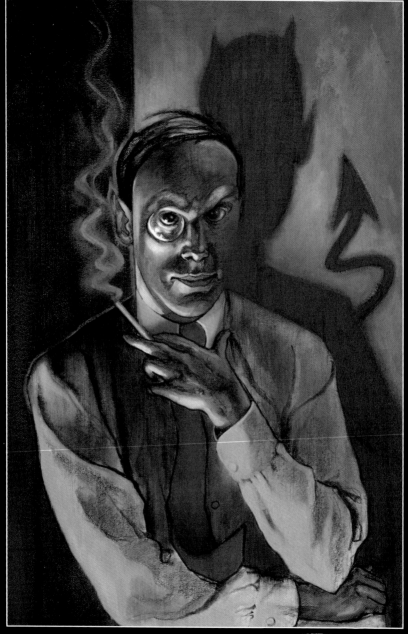

Jim DeLapine

Art Available On Macintosh
398 31st. Street · Lindenhurst NY 11757
(516) 225-1247

LANE DUPONT 203-222-1562
20 EVERGREEN AVE., WESTPORT, CT 06880
FAX 203-222-0080

DEBORAH DUTKO
286 MOHEGAN ROAD, HUNTINGTON, CT 06484
(203) 925-0878

CAROL GILDAR

FINE ART ILLUSTRATION
RSVP CALLBACK ANSWERING SERVICE: (718) 857-9267
FAX # UPON REQUEST

LAURIE HARDEN · ILLUSTRATOR

LAURIE HARDEN, 121 BANTA LANE, BOONTON, NJ 07005 (201) 335-4578
CLIENTS: GROSSET & DUNLAP, AMERICAN LUNG ASSOC., ABC, CBS, NJ BELL,
N.Y. TIMES, LADIES HOME JOURNAL, SCHOLASTIC, RED BOOK, TIME INC.

Janice Fried

459 Ninth Street, Brooklyn, NY 11215 • Phone: 718-832-0881 • Fax: 718-832-0198

THE
ILLUSTRATOR
(804) 543-5373

MARK CAREY · 1114 VIRGINIA AVE CHESAPEAKE, VIRGINIA 23324

TEMPTATIONS
AT THE BEACH

TEMPTATIONS AT THE BEACH. MIXED MEDIA COLLAGE ON CLOTH: 74 X 76 INCHES.

CHRISTE
ILLUSTRATION AND DESIGN

212 - 222 - 2538

Deborah Haley Melmon

Represented by Sharon Morris Associates
580 Washington Street Suite 204 San Francisco, CA 94111
Phone 415.362.8280 Fax 415.362.8310

Judith Wood

Represented by Sharon Morris Associates
580 Washington Street Suite 204 San Francisco, CA 94111
Phone 415.362.8280 Fax 415.362.8310

CLAUDE MARTINOT

Wraping paper/ promotion ©1994 Claude Martinot

145 2ND AVENUE #20
NEW YORK N Y 10003
(212) 473-3137
STUDIO: 1133 BROADWAY #1614
NEW YORK N Y 10010
(212) 645-0097 FAX: (212) 691-3657

GECKO ISLAND

CLAUDE MARTINOT

145 2ND AVENUE #20
NEW YORK N Y 10003
(212) 473-3137
STUDIO: 1133 BROADWAY #1614
NEW YORK N Y 10010
(212) 645-0097 FAX: (212) 691-3657

" I bring a lot of fun to every project. My clients keep calling because they know I respect my deadlines, but also because we laugh a lot and have a good time."

From ART DIRECTION MAGAZINE/ February 1994
©1994 Claude Martinot

deb hoeffner ___ soft realism

201-838-5490 538 Cherry Tree Lane, Kinnelon, NJ 07405

DICK
FLOOD

Represented by Sell Inc.
(312) 578-8844
FAX (312) 578-8847

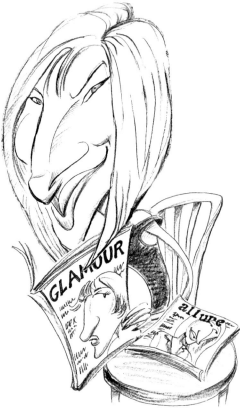

Laurie Edmonds illustration

RSVP callback

(718) 857-9267

CARICATURE
and
HUMOROUS
ILLUSTRATION

STORYBOARDS

Bruce Rauffenbart
COMPS
STORYBOARDS
ANIMATICS

Tel 212 924-2771

ART FOR PRESENTATION AND TESTING.
ARCHITECTURAL, EXHIBIT, PRODUCT
AND CONCEPTUAL RENDERING.

170 WEST 23RD STREET, #4E
NEW YORK, NY 10011
FAX 212 366-5850

CLIENTS INCLUDE:
ABSOLUT, AT&T, BMW,
EPCOT CENTER,
HASBRO, IBM,
XEROX

MPS

ANIMATICS

A wise, hilarious, offbeat novel of

Contemporary relationships and human foibles

JOHN HOLDER

Represented By **PHILIP M. VELORIC**

128 BEECHTREE DRIVE, BROOMALL, PA 19008

PHONE: (610) 356-0362 • FAX: (610) 353-7531

LANE YERKES

Represented By PHILIP M. VELORIC

128 BEECHTREE DRIVE, BROOMALL, PA 19008
PHONE: (610) 356-0362 • FAX: (610) 353-7531

DON DYEN

Represented By PHILIP M. VELORIC

128 BEECHTREE DRIVE, BROOMALL, PA 19008
PHONE: (610) 356-0362 • FAX: (610) 353-7531

1891

HEIGHTS

HOUSTON

206

1991

STEPHEN WELLS

Represented By **PHILIP M. VELORIC**

128 BEECHTREE DRIVE, BROOMALL, PA 19008
PHONE: (610) 356-0362 • FAX: (610) 353-7531

195

Specializing in
diagrams, charts
and maps created
on the Macintosh

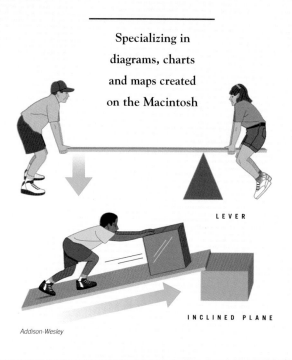

LEVER

INCLINED PLANE

Addison-Wesley

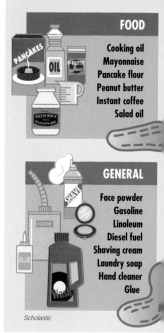
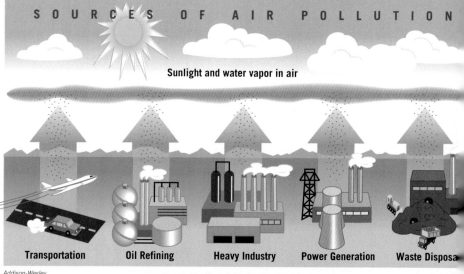

SOURCES OF AIR POLLUTION

Sunlight and water vapor in air

Transportation   Oil Refining   Heavy Industry   Power Generation   Waste Disposal

Addison-Wesley

NINA WALLACE

Represented By **PHILIP M. VELORIC**
128 BEECHTREE DRIVE, BROOMALL, PA 19008
PHONE: (610) 356-0362 • FAX: (610) 353-7531

KAREL HAYES

Represented By PHILIP M. VELORIC

128 BEECHTREE DRIVE, BROOMALL, PA 19008
PHONE: (610) 356-0362 • FAX: (610) 353-7531

Rick Brown

Phone/Fax (215) 794-8186
4290 Upper Mt. Rd./P.O. BOX 341 FURLONG, PA. 18925

FRANK R. SOFO ILLUSTRATION
16 BRANCH LANE, LEVITTOWN, N.Y. 11756 (516) 681-8745
RSVP CALLBACK ANSWERING SERVICE (718) 857-9267

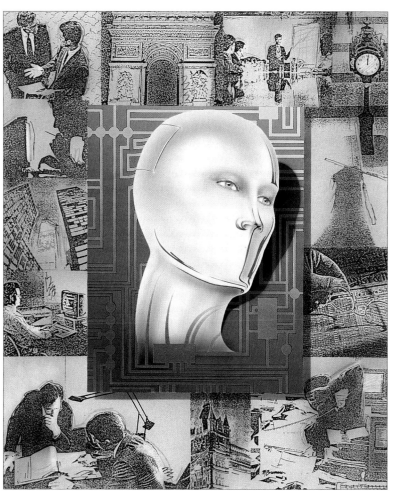

Mark
Bremmer
303
932.8759

SHAWN BANNER

53 Duncan Ave #56 • Jersey City, NJ 07304 • 201 333 6652

McCash
illustration

Trudy Sands, Artist Representative
1350 Chemical Street, Dallas, Tx. 75207

214-905-9037 • Fax 214-905-9038 • Studio 713-799-2279

Michael Annino
7082551359
RSVP CallBack Answering Service
7188579267

LORI NELSON FIELD
2ol 783 1321

Katie Keller---- 718-522-2334

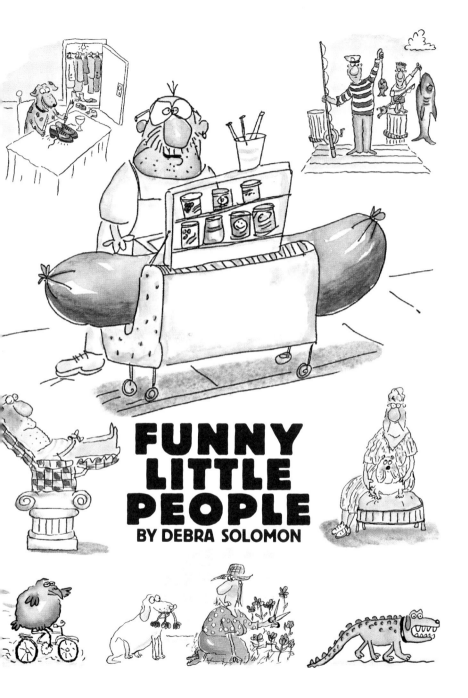

FUNNY LITTLE PEOPLE
BY DEBRA SOLOMON

(ANIMALS ALWAYS AVAILABLE)

43 GREENE STREET APT. 3 NEW YORK, NY 10012 TEL. (212) 473-0060 FAX (212) 473-7163

EMMA CRAWFORD

GRAPHIC ILLUSTRATION & DESIGN

212.260.2244

H O L L Y   S T O N E

(504) 273–0257
RSVP CALLBACK ANSWERING SERVICE (718) 857–9267

1·800·
DRAWS
·4·
⌣
〰〰〰
7¹8·499·
4006

DANIEL
ABRAHAM

 **_Laura LoTurco_**
_(718) 858-2413_

6 Pierrepont Street, 1B • Brooklyn, New York 11201

...THE DAY DUBINSKY HAD ENOUGH OF LARRY.

DIGITAL ILLUSTRATION
AND CHARACTER
DEVELOPMENT FOR THE
YOUTH MARKET
914-993-0859
914-962-0526

BOB BERRY ILLUSTRATION & DESIGN INC.
296 NORTH CENTRAL AVENUE APT 2A HARTSDALE, NY 10530

PAUL FISCH

5111 COFFEE TREE LANE N SYRACUSE NY 13212 (315) 451-8147

ROSE MARY BERLIN
Berlin Productions Inc.
870 Locke Lane, Yorktown Hts., NY 10598
(914) 962-0526   (914) 962-0174 Fax

JOIN OUR BOOK PARADE

Susan Banta

Illustration

(617) 876-8568

17 Magazine Street, Cambridge, MA 02139

Barbara Gray Illustrations
phone & fax: (212) 288-3938

Foca Company
NUTRITIONAL LABELS

The City Bakery
3-D WINDOW DISPLA

NYC Ballet
NUTCRACKER MOVIE

JANE SANDER.
ILLUSTRATION
212-986-1827

ARTIST AGENT
· JEAN CONLON ·
212-966-9897

Nickelodeon Magazine
ANNOYING PET SONG CONTEST

EVAN POLENGHI
STUDIO
718·499·3214

ARTIST AGENT
JEAN CONLON
212·966·9891

Electronic art for Paramount Publishing

ANNA VELTFORT
16 WEST 86 STREET, #B, NEW YORK, NY 10024
(212) 877-0430

"...ks like another blizzard of statistics!"

KAREN LEON

154-01 BARCLAY AVENUE, FLUSHING, NY 11355 (718) 461-2050, (718) 463-3159. FAX AVAILABLE.
Illustration, Humor & Editorial Cartoons, Caricatures & Storyboards.

CLIENTS: Federal Express, Playboy Enterprises Inc., National Hockey League, American Express, Panasonic, Ladies Home Journal, The Wall Street Journal, Public Relations Society of America, EMI Records, Miramax Films, Rockport Shoe Company, Champion International Corporation, International Chronometrics Corp., Brooks Pharmacy, Army Magazine, Emergency Medicine News.

223

EMILY THOMPSON

433 West 43rd Street #3E NYC 10036
Phone & Fax 212.245.2543
RSVP Callback answering service 718.857.9267

Lauren Klementz-Harte
(203) 235-6145

225

pictures by
Dorothy Stott

RSVP Callback Answering Service (718) 857-9267

Client List includes:
Dutton Children's Books
The Putnam & Grosset Group
Little, Brown & Co.

Children's Television Network
Silver Burdett Ginn
Harcourt Brace & Co.
Scott Foresman

Peter Church

REPRESENTED BY **CAROL BANCROFT & FRIENDS** (203) 438-8386

227

Nancy Mantha

REPRESENTED BY CAROL BANCROFT & FRIENDS (203) 438-8386

ANN BARROW

REPRESENTED BY **CAROL BANCROFT FRIENDS** (203) 438-8386

Carole Katchen

Don Weller

REPRESENTED BY **CAROL BANCROFT & FRIENDS** (203) 438-8386

Shelley Dieterichs

REPRESENTED BY **CAROL BANCROFT & FRIENDS** (203) 438-8386

REPRESENTED BY CAROL BANCROFT & FRIENDS (203) 438-8386

David Melendez

REPRESENTED BY   CAROL BANCROFT & FRIENDS   (203) 438-8386

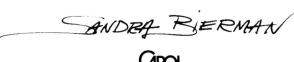

SANDRA BIERMAN

REPRESENTED BY (203) 438-8386

235

DESIGN

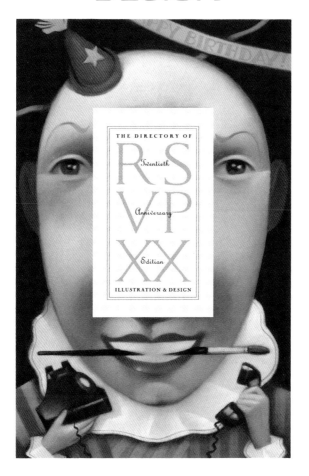

THE DIRECTORY OF

R S
V P
X X

Twentieth

Anniversary

Edition

ILLUSTRATION & DESIGN

LOUISE FILI LTD DESIGNS:

BOOKS, BOOK JACKETS, LOGOS,

RESTAURANT IDENTITIES,

PACKAGING, PROMOTION AND

POSTERS. PORTFOLIO AVAILABLE

ON REQUEST. 71 FIFTH AVENUE

NEW YORK CITY, NEW YORK 10003

TEL: 212 989-9153   FAX: 212 989-1453

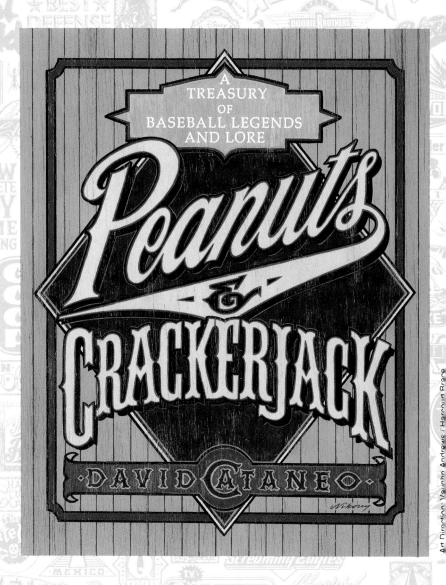

A TREASURY
OF
BASEBALL LEGENDS
AND LORE

Peanuts

&

CRACKERJACK

·DAVID CATANE·

Art Direction: Vaughn Andrews / Harcourt Brace

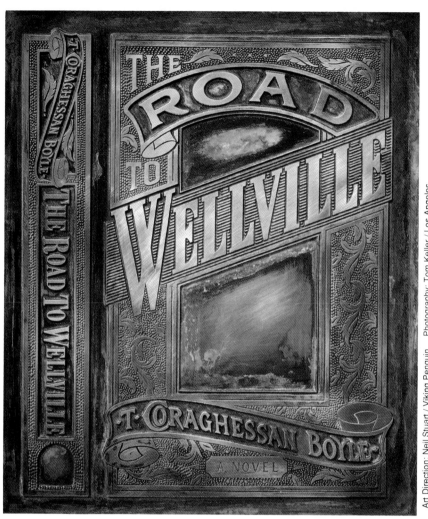

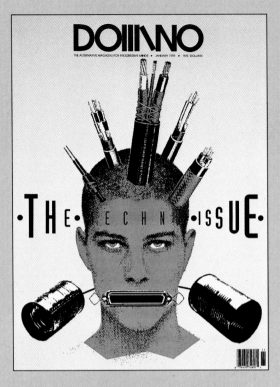

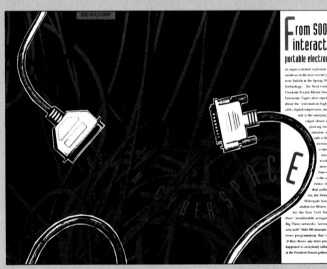

rodrigo peña >designer

ANAHEIM

HISTOR...

NEW ENGLAND

OCEAN SIDE

SAN DIEGO
SAN DIEGO

CHULA VISTA

GREETINGS FROM THE

NORTHEAST

SANTA ROSA
SANTA ROSA

THE ANAGRAM DESIGN GROUP,
LOGOS, DESIGN & ILLUSTRATION
METICULOUSLY CRAFTED.

CARMINE VECCHIO • 718 • 848-6176

Checking steam system components

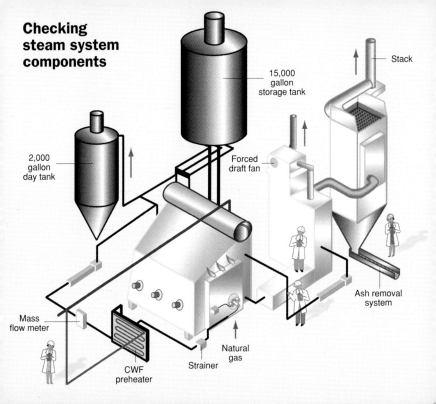

15,000 gallon storage tank

Stack

2,000 gallon day tank

Forced draft fan

Mass flow meter

CWF preheater

Strainer

Natural gas

Ash removal system

Poverty Rates for Black Children

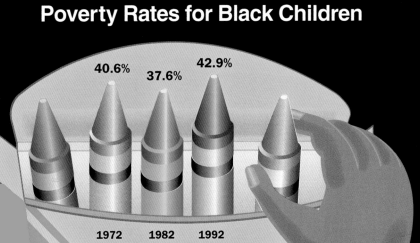

40.6% 37.6% 42.9%

1972 1982 1992

Year

U.S. Bureau of the Census, 1993

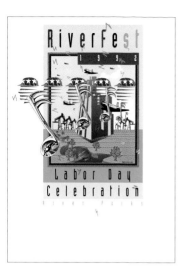

MARTIN
COLLIER
DIGITAL DESIGN & ILLUSTRATION
214. 987. 3952

RSVP Callback Answering Service 718. 857. 9267

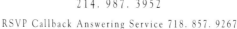

GRAPHIC CHART & MAP CO., INC.

State Beer Exercise Taxes

Highest States

Second-Highest

Middle States

Second-Lowest

Lowest States

WA-15¢
OR-8¢
ID-15¢
MT-18¢
WY-2¢
ND-16¢
SD-27¢
MN-15¢
WI-6¢
MI-20¢
NV-9¢
UT-35¢
CO-8¢
NE-23¢
IA-19¢
IL-7¢
IN-12¢
OH-11¢
NY-21¢
PA-8¢
NH-35¢
VT-27¢
MA-11¢
RI-10¢
CT-19¢
NJ-16¢
DE-16¢
MD-9¢
DC-9¢
CA-20¢
AZ-16¢
NM-18¢
KS-18¢
MO-6¢
KY-8¢
WV-18¢
VA-26¢
TN-13¢
NC-48¢
SC-77¢
OK-40¢
AR-31.5¢
MS-43¢
AL-53¢
GA-48¢
TX-19¢
LA-32¢
FL-48¢
AK-35¢
HI-89¢ *

SOURCES

The Tobacco Institute.
Tax Burden on Tobacco:
Historical Compilation. Vol. 27.
Washington, DC, 1994. p.viii

+6 +8 +10 +12 +10 +8

ARCTIC OCEAN

+13

ASIA

NORTH PACIFIC OCEAN

SEOUL
SHANGHAI
SHENZHEN
TOKYO
TAIPEI
HONG KONG
MANILA
+5½
BOMBAY
+6½
BANGKOK
COLOMBO
KUALA LUMPUR
SINGAPORE
JAKARTA

INDIAN OCEAN

+9½
AUSTRALIA
MELBOURNE
SYDNEY
AUCKLAND

+5 +7 +9 +11 +11 +9

Alcohol, Marijuana, and Cigarette Use, 1992-1993

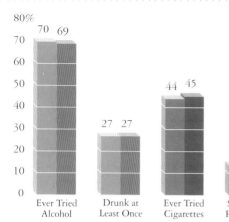

80%

- 70 (Ever Tried Alcohol, 1992)
- 69 (Ever Tried Alcohol, 1993)
- 27 (Drunk at Least Once, 1992)
- 27 (Drunk at Least Once, 1993)
- 44 (Ever Tried Cigarettes, 1992)
- 45 (Ever Tried Cigarettes, 1993)
- 14 (Smoked in Past Month, 1992)
- 16 (Smoked in Past Month, 1993)
- 10 (Ever Tried Marijuana, 1992)
- 11 (Ever Tried Marijuana, 1993)
- 3 (Smoked in Past Month, 1992)
- 4 (Smoked in Past Month, 1993)

Categories: Ever Tried Alcohol · Drunk at Least Once · Ever Tried Cigarettes · Smoked in Past Month · Ever Tried Marijuana · Smoked in Past Month

1992 — 1993

DESIGN

GRAPHIC
*Chart &
Map*
COMPANY, INC.

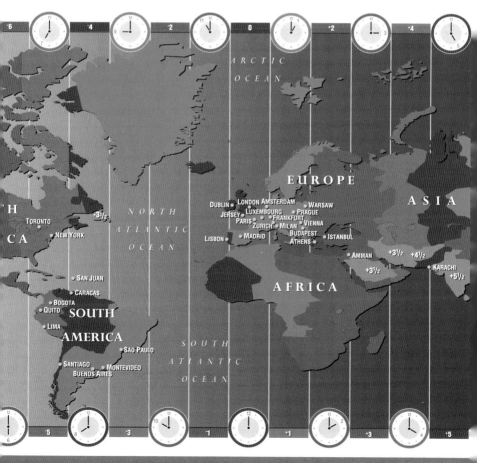

212.463.0190 / FAX.463.0510

© THE WALT DISNEY COMPANY.

PIG
TALES

PETER BELMONT
GOLF SCHOOL

Say Cheese Shops

BRAINTREE

BODKIN DESIGN GROUP

25 SYLVAN ROAD SOUTH, WESTPORT, CT 06880   203.221.0404

ILLUSTRATION

THE DIRECTORY OF

RSVP XX

Twentieth Anniversary Edition

ILLUSTRATION & DESIGN

GERRY GERSTEN

INTERMEDIAIR

VEY KAHN 212 752 8490   201 467 0223
FAX 201 467 5905

LAUREN SCHEUER

617-924-6799
77 PIERCE ROAD, WATERTOWN, MA 02172
SEE ALSO CREATIVE ILLUSTRATION BOOK

Detail from 48x48" display at
US POSTAL MUSEUM, in which
Senators Platt, DePew, Aldritch
(linked to RR express monopolies)
argue against parcel post service
proposed by Postmaster Gen.
(& mail order mogul)
John Wanamaker

Van Howell
516-424-6499
OR 212-517-1460
Box 812, Huntington NY 11743

See also RSVP 13 to 19

Right: Portrait of Edna Foa
Prentice-Hall 1994

David Chelsea

43 WEST 27TH ST. 9R NEW YORK NY 10001
(212) 889-6196 FAX: (212) 684-8089

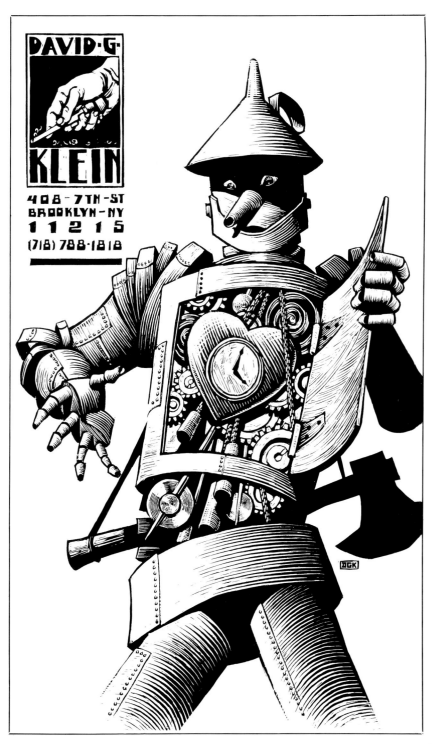

Richard Lebenson

253 WASHINGTON AVENUE, BROOKLYN, N.Y. 11205 (718) 857-9267

The Universe Makers

SCIENCE FICTION TODAY

Richard Lebenson

253 WASHINGTON AVENUE, BROOKLYN, N.Y. 11205 (718) 857-9267

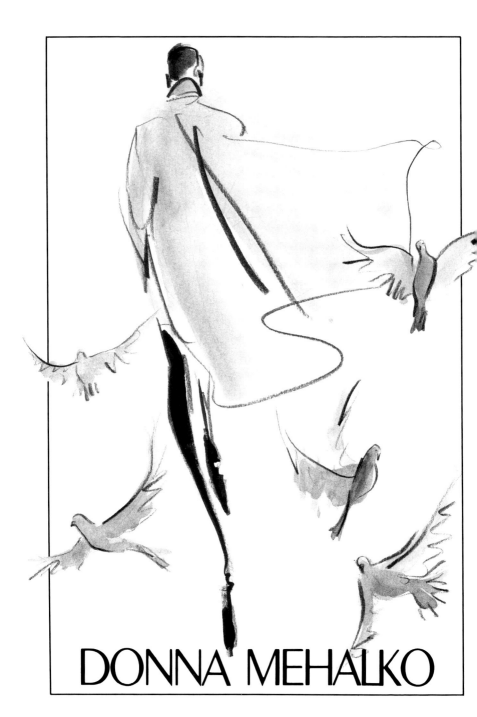

DONNA MEHALKO

515 EAST 82ND STREET • #5C
NEW YORK, NEW YORK 10028
PHONE/FAX 212 • 794 • 6297

STEPHEN HARRINGTON

255 WILTON ROAD WEST · RIDGEFIELD · CT · 06877
(203) 431· 5854
REPRESENTED BY JOHN BREWSTER CREATIVE SERVICES

Leo Bliok

990 Ave. of the Americas,
New York, NY 10018 · Suite 16 S

Illustration & Caricature

Studio: 212-629-8559 · Home: 516-466-8879

ANGELO

ARTIST/ILLUSTRATOR EXTRAORDINAIRE
1449 LONGFELLOW AVENUE • BRONX NY 10459 • (718) 617-2907
RSVP CALLBACK ANSWERING SERVICE (718) 857-9267

Richard Leonard
·MARTINEZ·

• LINE ART & WOODCUTS •
212 W. 17TH ST. #2B, N.Y.C. 10011
(212) 243–6613, RSVP CALLBACK (718) 857–9267

Marty Norman

(516) 671-4482

EXAMPLES OF RON BARRETT ILLUSTRATION AS USED IN EVERYDAY LIFE.

A. ON TV
Politenessman for
1-800- COLLECT

B. ON CD
Angel®

C. IN LIBRARIES
Cloudy With a Chance of Meatballs

D. ON NEWSSTAND
The New York Times

E. IN MUSEUM
The American Museum
of Natural History

Mark A Gallagher

R.S.V.P. call back (7¡8) 857*9267

KEVIN SPARROCK
ILLUSTRATOR
2520 KENNEDY BOULEVARD
#5H JERSEY CITY, NJ 07304
2 0 1 • 9 1 5 • 0 7 3 0

HOW TO MAKE A CARTOON

COME UP WITH AN IDEA...

LAYOUT YOUR TOOLS...

DEVELOP YOUR CHARACTERS...

AND AVOID~

TRAPS...

TYPOS...

& DELAYS!

LEO ABBETT CARTOONS 269 MASON TERR. BROOKLINE, MA. 02146
PHONE & FAX 617·566·2893 · MEMBER GRAPHIC ARTISTS GUILD

271

LAURIE HARDEN, 121 BANTA LANE, BOONTON, NJ 07005 (201) 335-4578
CLIENTS: GROSSET & DUNLAP, AMERICAN LUNG ASSOC., ABC, CBS, NJ BELL,
N.Y. TIMES, LADIES HOME JOURNAL, SCHOLASTIC, RED BOOK, TIME INC.

HIROHITO

Kevin Stone

14 St. James Place. Brooklyn, NY 11205
(718) 857-2418

ART GLAZER
2 JAMES ROAD, MT. KISCO, N.Y. 10549
(914) 666-4554

PAULA L. WINTERS PH/FAX 305·927·9735

TRISH BURGIO

(310)657-1469

RSVP CALLBACK ANSWERING SERVICE   (718)857-9267

MAC NEILL *and* MAC INTOSH

74 YORK STREET
LAMBERTVILLE NJ 08530
609·397·4631
CALL FOR
FLOPPY PORTFOLIO

USAir Magazine
Dallas, Texas Trolley

Computer Shopper
Laptop Computers Go Traveling

Hewlett Packard
1993 Open Migration Program

V.G. MYERS
HUMOROUS ILLUSTRATION & CARICATURES
41 DOUGLAS ROAD • GLEN RIDGE, NJ 07028 • 201-429-8131 PHONE & FAX

MICHAEL DAVID BIEGEL ILLUSTRATION (201) 825-0084

Elizabeth Williams
212.945.6442

Clients include: The New York Times, N.W. Ayer,
Ammirati & Puris, Newsday, Houghton Mifflin,
ABC Sports, Scholastic, Oxford University Press

Andrea Geller

8B Daisy Way, Paramus, NJ 07652   201·843·0228

JERRY GONZALEZ
DESIGN & COMPUTER ILLUSTRATION
(718) 204-8762

SUSAN DETRICH · ILLUSTRATION

253 BALTIC STREET • BROOKLYN NEW YORK 11201 • 718-237-9174
FOR ADDITIONAL WORK SEE RSVP 16 • 17 • 18 • 19 • CREATIVE ILLUSTRATION BOOK 1991
GAG DIRECTORY OF ILLUSTRATION 5 • 6 • 8 • 9 • 10 & AMERICAN SHOWCASE 18

SUSAN·FOX
ILLUSTRATION
DESIGN·LETTERING
707·443·1427

GORILLA

PEACE on EARTH

BIG BEN & WESTMISTER BRIDGE

EUREKA

Dawn Albore
24 Hillside Ave., Montclair, NJ 07042 (201) 744-9188

DESIGN

THE DIRECTORY OF

RSVP XX

Twentieth

Anniversary

Edition

ILLUSTRATION & DESIGN

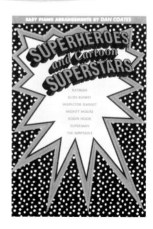

55 Park Avenue, New York 10016 (212) 750-2191 Fax (212) 750-0891

Desktop Publishing, Computer Generated Art, Advertising, Logos, Brochures, Promotional Materials, Catalogs, Manuals, Direct Mail and Outdoor Billboards.

JULIAN WATERS

Morning Milking
LINDA LOWE MORRIS · DAVID DERAN

Distinguished Advertisers Club
C&P YELLOW PAGES

Hawaii's Alluring
Orchids

The National Symphony Orchestra Ball 1990

Relationships

The Speedball Textbook
22ND EDITION · FOR PEN AND BRUSH LETTERING · NEW AND IMPROVED!

ABCD EFGHI JKLM NOPQ RSTUV WXYZ

The Bismarck Found

Baby Love

Share Your Blessings

Good Morning Good Night
Ivan Gantschev

El Fuego

MASTERS of TRADITIONAL ARTS

Coastland Center

Royalties

Ghosts
OF THE PAST

Get Motivated

The Words We Live By.

(301) 253-3422 ❧ **FAX 972-2271**
Award-winning hand lettering for headlines, logos, advertising, typefaces, etc
VERSATILITY IN STYLE USING PEN, BRUSH AND MACINTOSH COMPUTER

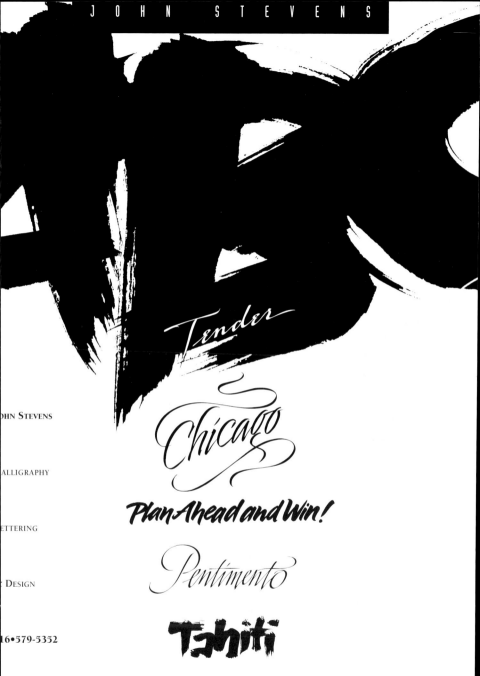

OHN STEVENS

ALLIGRAPHY

ETTERING

DESIGN

16•579-5352

AX 735-6535

Tender

Chicago

Plan Ahead and Win!

Pentimento

Tahiti

Silk Reflections

Pretty

the wave

SEASONINGS

WHEN YOU LOSE SIMPLICITY YOU LOSE DRAMA — WYETH

Heart Songs

GUESS WHO'S DATING A WEREWOLF?

NINETEEN HUNDRED '94

THEATRE Virginia

Quixotic

Beethoven

Guam Museum

Michael Clark Design
Contemporary Lettering, Calligraphy and Type Design
RSVP Callback Answering Service (718) 857-9267

TONY DI SPIGNA DESIGN
(718) 837-2204 or (516) 281-6706

CORPORATE IDENTITIES • SYMBOLS • LOGOTYPES • EXCLUSIVE TYPEFACES
ALL STYLES OF LETTERFORM & TYPOGRAPHIC DESIGN
RSVP CALLBACK ANSWERING SERVICE (718) 857-9267

FOR LOGOS,
LETTERING,
DESIGN AND
ILLUSTRATION
METICULOUSLY
CRAFTED.

LOGOS,
LETTERING,
DESIGN
AND
ILLUSTRATION
TASTFULLY
CONCEIVED,
MACINTOSH
EXECUTED.

CARMINE VECCHIO • **ANAGRAM DESIGN** • **718 848-6176**

At Your Fingertips!

A Chelsea Evening

Cafe Nicholson

This is the life!

Farewell to Siena
A NOVEL

Big

Arianna Marie

World Series

Unforgettably Yours

שטר

New York Shopping Spree

A.P.A W.L.I.

AWARD-WINNING HAND LETTERING AND GRAPHIC DESIGN SOLUTIONS
TRADITIONAL AND MACINTOSH COMPUTER ENHANCED.

Rappy & Company

150 West 22nd Street, 10th Floor
New York, New York 10011
Tel: 212.989.0603 Fax: 212.989.0419

298

SHORE 94 GUIDE

ARETHA FRANKLIN

The Delaware NEW JERSEY'S WEST COAST

A Holiday of Love

TABO

A Beautiful Feast for a Big King Cat

PREGNANT PAUSES

Lebbad

JAMES A. LEBBAD
609·737·3458   212·645·5260
GRAPHIC AND TYPOGRAPHIC DESIGN
BY MAC OR BY HAND

299

The Castle

Frümash's Pottery

Meteors

Monster Museum

Re-Cycle

Trapped in a Two-Dimensional World

Los Vatos
and the Cholo Girls

Madonna

Grace
Under Fire

I DONT CARE
ABOUT the WORLD

Reebok
for
Kids

The shortest distance to a whole new look isn't a straight line. It's Lots of curly ones.

JILL BELL
DESIGN AND LETTERING

———

HAND LETTERING
CALLIGRAPHIC LOGOTYPES
MAC MANIPULATIONS
& OTHER COOL STUFF

❖

Call for further samples

310 372-4204

LOS ANGELES

the
Old World
in a
New Way

Paloma
Picasso

A Little Princess

SISTER OF PAIN

Bark Cloth Basket Weave Bird's Eye
canvas Cord Crinkled Georgette Crepe
Crochet Checky Weaves Chevron Distress
Grass Cloth Herringbone Hopsack
Lace Linen Pucker Rib Sheer
Sheeting Textured Rayon Thermal

SCAR

301

INDEX

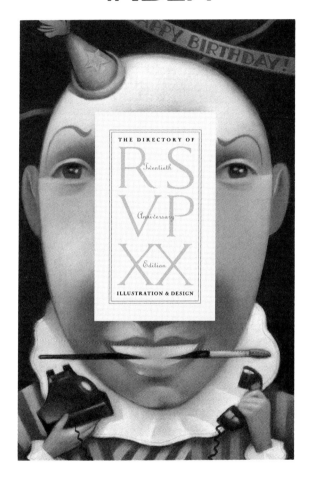

INDEX

ILLUSTRATION

*RSVP CallBack answering service (718) 857-9267

INDEX

*RSVP CallBack answering service (718) 857-9267

INDEX

*RSVP CallBack answering service (718) 857-9267

INDEX

*RSVP CallBack answering service (718) 857–9267

INDEX

FASHION ILLUSTRATION/ACCESSORIES

3D ILLUSTRATION

COLLAGE

SILHOUETTES & CUT–OUTS

WOOD–CUTS/SCRATCHBOARD

CARTOONING/HUMOROUS

*RSVP CallBack answering service (718) 857–9267

INDEX

*RSVP CallBack answering service (718) 857–9267

INDEX

*RSVP CallBack answering service (718) 857–9267

INDEX

ARCHITECTURAL RENDERING & ILLUSTRATION

TECHNICAL RENDERING & PRODUCT ILLUSTRATION

SCIENTIFIC ILLUSTRATION

CHARTS & MAPS

COMPUTER ART

*RSVP CallBack answering service (718) 857–9267

INDEX

ARTISTS REPRESENTATIVES

GRAPHIC DESIGN

*RSVP CallBack answering service (718) 857–9267

INDEX

LETTERING, LOGOS & CALLIGRAPHY

ART DIRECTION

PACKAGE DESIGN

HAND–PAINTED PHOTOGRAPHY

*RSVP CallBack answering service (718) 857–9267

GEOGRAPHIC BREAKDOWN

GEOGRAPHIC BREAKDOWN

GEOGRAPHIC BREAKDOWN

WEST (AK AZ CA CO HI ID MT NV NM OR UT WA WY)

CANADA

ENGLAND

IF YOU CAN'T SEE

EYE to EYE

SEE US.

We're the Joint Ethics Committee — th
people to see when business problems ha
you and your client at odds.

Since 1945, the JEC has been meetin
monthly to act upon complaints and viol
tions of its Code of Fair Practice. We arbitra
solutions to business disputes and ethic
questions before they reach the often exa
perating realm of the courts.

And we do it very inexpensively. O
arbitrators are concerned, objective volu
teers from the advertising and graph
communication arts industries. They belie
fair business dealings should be a right, n
a fight.

If it sounds like you need our help, plea
write to us at P.O. Box 179, Grand Central St
tion, New York, NY 10163. Describe the pro
lem you're having. Let's see what we can d

To start a JEC chapter in your state: Request our brochu
"How to Establish a Joint Ethics Committee". For a copy of
Code of Fair Practice, please send five dollars.

J O I N T   E T H I C S   C O M M I T T E

YOU DON'T HAVE TO KNOW ALL THE RIGHT PEOPLE. JUST AS LONG AS YOU KNOW US.

Whether you are an art director, a designer, artist or photographer, your most important contact is a SPAR rep.

We represent the best illustrators and photographers in the business. SPAR reps do it better than anyone because we're professionals who get to know you as well as the artists and photographers we represent. We handle each assignment personally and efficiently from start to finish, saving you time, effort and money.

A SPAR rep is the single, easiest way to make all the contacts you need. Give us a call. We'll introduce you to all the right people.

SOCIETY OF PHOTOGRAPHER AND ARTIST REPRESENTATIVES, INC.

Suite 1166, 60 East 42nd Street New York, NY 10165 212-822-1415

Membership directory, rep kit and portfolio reviews available. Newsletter ad rates upon request.

WHAT IS CALLBACK?

IF YOU'RE HAVING TROUBLE CONTACTING AN ARTIST IN RSVP, USE CALLBACK, OUR 24 HR., 7 DAY A WEEK, ANSWERING SERVICE. WE MAINTAIN DATABASE RECORDS OF ALL CHANGES OF ADDRESS AND PHONE NUMBER FOR PARTICIPATING ARTISTS. OUR STAFF RECEIVES YOUR CALL, RELAYS YOUR MESSAGE AND KEEPS A RUNNING RECORD OF ALL YOUR REFERRALS.

BACK EDITIONS

EACH ANNUAL EDITION OF RSVP FEATURES A COMPLETELY DIFFERENT SPECTRUM OF ARTISTS AND ARTWORK. BACK EDITIONS ARE AVAILABLE AT SPECIALLY REDUCED PRICES. ALL COPIES ARE BRAND NEW. QUANTITIES ARE LIMITED AND SOME EDITIONS ARE ALREADY OUT OF PRINT, SO PLEASE CONTACT US IMMEDIATELY FOR ORDERING INFORMATION.

TO ADVERTISE IN RSVP:

ANY ILLUSTRATOR, DESIGNER, PHOTOGRAPHER OR REP WANTING TO BE PLACED ON OUR MAILING LIST FOR INFORMATION ABOUT PAGE RATES, DEADLINES, ETC. IS ENCOURAGED TO CONTACT US AT 718/857-9267 OR RSVP: THE DIRECTORY OF CREATIVE TALENT, P.O. BOX 314, BROOKLYN, NEW YORK 11205